<u>CREATE THE CHAOS</u>

BY

JOE DUBIN

CHAPTER 1

What exactly is Create the Chaos? I am so glad you asked because I think with the power of prayer and a little direction and motivation, you can absolutely change your life for the better. Now I am not saying that you will go out in the next week and win the powerball, but hey if you do, we will share the credit.

Kidding but what you can take away from this might be much greater than winning said powerball. You will have power all right, but it will be your power that you created and then wonderful chaos. You will be amazed at how differently you see life and you will not look back.

Where did I get the idea for this? As with most things, I believe God speaks to us in wonderful and beautiful ways and we just have to listen. He certainly did that to me and once I finally shut down my bravado and humbled myself, the world became pretty cool.

One time playing football, I got double-teamed while on defense and they blocked me about fifteen yards down the field. I remember coming to the sideline and my coach saying, "Next time you feel that happening, fall down. Make a giant pile that makes it difficult for anyone to go through. Make it chaotic for the other team."

That moment has stayed with me my entire life but I put a different spin on it. As I was starting my broadcasting career, I was a cameraman, called photojournalist, and I wanted to do more things on air as a reporter. I sent out a ton of resume tapes and got back nothing from other TV stations and news directors. Nothing.

I was crushed until one day, this saying came to mind. The definition of insanity is doing the same thing over and over and expecting a different result. That was me! I was sending the same resume tape and expecting to get a job and that was not happening. I went back to work in my lab and did my resume tape in a completely different way that I made funny and exciting and it was under two minutes long, instead of the six minutes before.

I sent 8 tapes out with my new reel and I got four responses back. Three job offers and I was floored. I sat back and realized that I had created this chaos and it was perfect.

Let that sink in for a second. I created the chaos.

You see, chaos does not always have to be bad, especially when you have control and I needed to insert some positivity and energy in what I was doing and created that chaos that ultimately put me on the path I am on and I thank God for that every single day.

I could have stayed doing the same thing, letting two guys block me all the way down the field and sending the same resume tape out, or do something about it. Create an obstacle they couldn't get past and let it be a building block for your life.

I told my son the same thing as he now approaches his sophomore year in high school. Create chaos in things that you do that drives your passion whether it be singing, acting, playing football or whatever you want to do. Create chaos that is wonderful and powerful that when you walk into the room, people immediately take notice.

My son and daughter know that one of the things in this world that really irks me is laziness. Simply no excuse for being lazy and that is why creating that chaos is so important to what I want them to do in life. My daughter created chaos by graduating from nursing school, passing her boards and getting hired as an R.N. It certainly was not easy but she busted her tail in accomplishing everything and I am over the moon proud of her.

Go ahead and create that chaos in your life. Go for that job you want. Go for three jobs that you want. Go on that vacation you have been wanting to go on. Just go and do it. Get involved in many things that you are passionate about.

Don't let the negativity stop you from being incredible. God wants us all to succeed and has given us some wonderful tools within ourselves to do that.

Create the chaos and never look back.

CHAPTER 2

Now creating that chaos is a beautiful thing but we also need to condition our mind and our body to think positive and great thoughts as much as we can. I know that is sometimes overwhelming in today's world but we got this and we got this together.

I want to introduce you to a game my son and I played when he was in elementary school that just oozes positivity when you adjust your eyes ever so slightly.

For twenty-five years, I worked in local news in Nashville. I tried every day to bring positivity to my stories but unfortunately some bosses and consultants think that is a bad thing. So "Just Count All The Red Cars" came out of this.

"That all sounds great but really, no one cares."

Actual words spoken to me by a former boss when I told him I was going to focus on as many positive stories as I could as we entered 2021. 2020 with covid was brutal in so many ways for so many people but those stories were out there and I was determined to find as many as I could.

I wasn't sure he heard me correctly, so I repeated what I said.

I was met with a shoulder shrug and a smirk.

I knew then what my focus was as my time at a certain TV station was coming to an end. Even as my former boss was cutting my time on the small screen down, I was going to find a way to keep these stories coming and coming.

I know, it might seem like a tall task but I had a moment with my son from years ago that I knew I could fall back on.

A teacher had given him a challenge in elementary school and he was only to count as many red cars as he could in an afternoon.

"Daddy, that is 14 and there is 15. Oh, wait, 16." And on and on and on. I forget exactly how many we counted that afternoon, but it was a lot.

Just count all the red cars.

What I discovered that afternoon is that we focus on one certain thing, we can block a lot of things out. Negative things. It was pretty easy. We focused only on red cars and that was it.

Now apply that to positive stories. It works and it works perfectly. You focus on one positive and then, another one pops up. Then another one. And another one. Quickly, you have a stable of positive stories that can be told.

I have applied this little game to so many facets of my life. Just focus on the good things and if you can't find it, search, and it will be there.

As I have said before, it takes the same amount of energy to focus on the bad as it does the good.

Just count all the red cars.

CHAPTER 3

One of my favorite things to do while watching a movie, is pull out my phone and hit my app for IMDB. It is one of the best apps and websites you will ever come across. Every single movie, actor, director, etc., is all listed there with some incredible information you might not have ever known.

I call it my "deep dive," when I am on searching through it which oftentimes leads into the one word we all know so well, wormhole.

It is where you are reading about something, then click on something that is linked to that, then you find yourself clicking on yet something else and before you know it, you are in a place that even Google Maps would say, "You're on your own with this one. Good luck."

Recently, and I don't even remember the starting point, (see paragraph above), I got lost in that dang wormhole and landed on a thread of improving your life, which I have written about quite a bit on here. It led me to a Greek philosopher named Epictetus, who taught that all men are the sons of God and He has given us a will to govern our own thoughts.

Then I read this that stopped me in my tracks:

"God has already given us everything we need to succeed; we only need to look within ourselves."

Powerful!

Again, few things make me pause and stand up and go take a walk and this did. Amazingly strong and simple. We can change the direction of a car by simply turning the steering wheel. We are the steering wheel. We are the driver and we can find our way on our own, and we do not need to go and purchase a brand new car, when the one we have is fine and all it needs is a tune-up.

I know a lot of us will make resolutions for the upcoming year of getting in shape, and being nicer, and doing more community work and on and on and on. If you truly want to do that, you can read all the books you want and talk to all the people you want, but if you don't put that one foot in front of the other, it really rings hollow.

If you really want that change, it starts inside of you and the tools are already there.

Thank you, wormhole, you finally made me feel as if I was not wasting my time, for once.

CHAPTER 4

Recently, I was tagged in a picture on Instagram and naturally, was intrigued so I went and clicked on the pic. Did not recognize the name nor did the person look familiar.

I was even more intrigued now so I continued reading and came upon this paragraph.

Fast forward to June 2020 - I saw Dani D. Fitness on News Channel 4 - @wsmv I loved her energy and her body positive message. It was all the motivation I needed. I messaged her, and I have now been her client for over a year and a half.

Ah, it all made sense now.

During covid, I came up with a segment each week on TV called, Workout Wednesday. We would visit area gyms and check in on trainers and people working out in these unprecedented times and see how things are going.

The trainer on TV this particular morning was Dani Dyer, better known as Dani D. Fitness. I had seen her before when I was co-hosting another show and she was completely fantastic so I wanted her to come on.

The segment was fun and we had a nice crowd who showed up in Cool Springs that morning and in doing those, you really never know who is watching but a big part of you is hoping someone sees these fun and positive stories and it inspires them.

This particular day, it was a lady named Wendy who happened to be tuning in. She was unhappy with her journey and realized that staying on that couch was only going to get worse. She decided to change that. She decided to take action and that is what this next paragraph is all about.

I have often said that the journey of a thousand miles begins with the first step when it comes to anything and Wendy, did just that. I have these three words written in every journal that I have, and I post it where I can see it. They are, Make It Happen.

It literally applies to everything that you are doing to improve your life. I can tell you go to workout and eat better all day long, but until you make it happen, it won't. And never will. No matter how much you want it to.

When I went back to college and graduated at 28, there was a guy in one of my classes who wanted to be a physical therapist. He was two years older than me and one day, he said he was going to drop out.

"Why are you wanting to drop out?" I was massively curious.

"Because, by the time it is all done, I will be 35."

I looked at him and said, "Let me ask. You plan on being 35 anyway don't you?"

Make it happen.

Do what Wendy did, and take that first step and my goodness, where you can and will go will amaze you for the rest of your life.

CHAPTER 5

This new year's resolution is so easy, it is almost too hard to believe. It costs nothing, you don't have to go anywhere and will make you feel so much better.

How about in 2022 let us celebrate others' success, more than our own. I know, crazy idea but let's try it and see what happens.

I am not talking about going way overboard and making it seem sarcastic but 100% genuine.

For example, there is a friend of mine who is always posting his son's athletic accomplishments and he said one time, "Sorry for all the posting but so proud of him." He felt the need to apologize for his son and how well he was doing. I sent him a note and said, "Never apologize for success." He wrote back and said thanks that it meant a lot to him.

Remember, a rising tide raises all ships and it has become really rewarding celebrating others success when and wherever I can. Promotion, wedding, birth of a child, new job, etc., it really doesn't matter but Lord, a kind word does a ton.

A few years ago, I was fortunate enough to win my second EMMY award but I did not attend the ceremony so I had left a message with a co-worker if they didn't mind bringing the statue back to the station. They said sure and handed it to another co-worker who was coming to work the very next day and he said, "I am not taking that. It can stay here." When I found out who it was, I was not surprised. I just laughed.

Jealousy is a most powerful eight letter word that can cause a lot of damage to your body if you open the door and let it in. As I have said, it takes just as much energy to be negative as it does positive. I know, I was that person a long time ago that I now look back on and want to fight. Remember, you can't unscramble eggs so no sense in going back to fix something.

I now drop kind and encouraging words all over the place. It only takes seconds and I never thought it would feel that good to do it, yet it is amazing.

In fact, you will not even have to search out the good because it is all around us. You will just be more aware of it and hitting send, will never feel more powerful at any point in your life.

CHAPTER 6

A few weeks ago, my son's football team was playing a game in Chattanooga, about a 2 hour drive from the house. After the game, I kissed his head and told him I would see him back at school to pick him up.

I was exhausted and the only thing that keeps me awake on those drives is talk radio. I got in the car and thankfully, it has satellite radio and so I just spun the dial and said wherever it lands, that is what we listen to on the way back.

It stopped at channel 460. The Billy Graham channel. Which, before that Wheel of Fortune spin, had no idea that channel existed. My grandpa loved Billy Graham so I punched it in and listened.

Prior to that, I had been thinking about the word regret. A word that can wreck your life if you try. We all have regrets and some will stay with us the entire time we are alive.

I have seen this quote several times and it is so true when it comes to regret. "You'll just keep crashing if you never take your eyes off the rearview mirror." Much easier said than done. But, so true.

Here is the part of the night that gives me chills. Within :45 seconds of turning on the channel, Billy Graham's message on the radio was about regret. And he said this, which is one of the most powerful things I have ever heard. "No matter how hard you try, you can't unscramble eggs."

Chills. Literally moments after turning on a channel I had no idea existed, I hear, no matter how hard you try, you can't unscramble eggs.

I looked down at the speedometer and I was going 45 miles an hour. On the interstate. If you honked at a red mazda on I-24 west outside of Chattanooga, on a Friday night for going slow, that was me.

I finally got through Monteagle and was still listening to Billy Graham, this time from a sermon in Boston in the 1980's. His voice was powerful as always but I kept going back to those four words. You can't unscramble eggs.

I reflected back to certain times in my life where regret came into play. Being so stupid in certain things, not doing this or that, not working hard enough, not saying a kind word when I could have and on and on and on.

You can't unscramble eggs.

I got home that night, hung out with my son and went to bed. I thank God every night before I fall asleep on the blessings in my life. That night, I simply thanked Him for spinning a dial.

CHAPTER 7

By now in life, it is rare when we come across a quote from someone that stops us in our tracks and makes us think about something else.

I am sure if I sat down and thought really hard, I could remember a few but it still is a rarity. That is why a quote I heard from a retiring NFL player hit me right in the chest and hard.

Danny Amendola played 14 seasons in the league and recently announced his retirement. He won two Super Bowls and what makes it all the more impressive is that he was not drafted. He had to basically walk-on with an NFL team and make it. In case you didn't know, that success rate is lower than one percent.

He is an amazing story of never quitting even after he was told to quit, many times. He stuck with it and is now saying goodbye on his terms.

This is the quote that got me. When asked why he is not playing anymore, he replied, "It was better than I could have ever imagined."

Let's read that again.

It was better than I could have ever imagined.

What if we could say that about half of the things in our life. Heck, maybe a third. Apply it to something simple like your garden. "Hey Susan, how is the garden coming along?" "Oh my, it is better than I could have ever imagined."

Let's try it for a vacation. Or a movie. Or an old car you recently purchased. A blind date. Your grandma's old recipe for fudge. Just keep going with it and it just makes me smile in every way possible.

As I kept coming up with situations, one came to me out of the blue and I am sure it was not by accident. Now this one made me smile. One of a journey that was so perfect and wonderful, you have to tell someone at the end of said journey. What will you say in the moment? I got mine now.

You approach the pearly gates and there is St. Peter. He asks you how it was on earth. You look at him and smile and say, "It was better than I could have ever imagined."

Amen.

CHAPTER 8

This past year, I ran my 15th half-marathon. Now, I don't write that to hear, "great job, Joe." Oh no. It is much grander than that. On this same Saturday, someone who has been training for months and months will also run in the half-marathon. Not just that one person, but many will be making their way through the streets of Nashville and wonder to themselves as they hit mile 8 with 5 more to go, "can I finish? Was it worth it? Why am I doing this?"

I will tell you why. Same reason I ran the first one and the same reason I will run five of these in 2022. All because I was told, many times, that you can't do it. That you are too fat and won't make a mile. That you are wasting your time. You name the put down, I probably heard it.

Let's go back to the "you can't do it," for a second. Those words came from people that I considered good friends and yes, I know some were probably joking but it absolutely fueled me in amazing ways. Other first time marathon runners have told me that no one believed in them and self-doubt called them more than the car warranty people. As I have often said, take the "t" out of "can't" and it changes how you approach everything. Everything.

I tell people that you will think about quitting at least 13 times because that is how many miles are in a half-marathon. Then I tell them, you see the end and this is where it gets spiritual. They ask what that is. I tell them that something happens to you when you cross that finish line. Something amazing happens to you and only you know what that is. It will happen again and again as you run more half-marathons but that first time, when you cross the line, it is an amazing feeling. You won't be able to describe it to those who have not done it, but you will know.

As I approached my first half back in 2005, I was given this great piece of advice before I crossed the starting line. It has stayed with me ever since and it is so simple, almost comical, but it was and has been massively powerful to me. Just run. That is it. Just run. Simple as can be and that makes it even better.

I wrote a few months ago that God has given us everything we need to succeed in anything we want to do and that part two of that is going out and making it happen. Go and make it happen. Those three words that I have written down in so many places. If you want to run a marathon, hike the Appalachian trail, climb a mountain, make it happen and go do it.

And when you cross that finish line, you will never be the same person that started that race, because something wonderful will happen inside of you.

Now just go run.

CHAPTER 9

Now this one might seem a little odd at first but once you read it and put it into context in improving your life, this makes so much sense.

I was never one for volunteering because I was told to never work for free. No matter what in your life, never work for free. We are taught that working for free is foolish and why in the world would you do that.

I will tell you why. It is therapeutic in so many ways. All you have to do is look around and there are some great opportunities. I am not saying work 40 hours a week for free, but time here and there will do wonders for your soul.

Now, I live in the great city of Nashville, Tennessee, and if you have seen the news or read on-line, everyone it seems is moving to Music City.

I say, come one and come all, to the greatest community in all of these beautiful United States.

I also have a little advice for you, and this is free and it is perfect. The best part is that it is so simple.

Get involved.

That is it, simply get involved.

I came from a place in my prior job where management couldn't tell you the difference between Gallatin or Galaga. Between Clarksville or Clark Kent. Between Murfreesboro and Murphy Fair.

They literally had no clue about the area and the wonderful people that make up all parts of it. Zero clue. (Also, note to bosses--Do NOT park in the first spot outside the office. That says all we need to know about you.)

But Joe, how do we get involved with so many things going on? Easy. Go talk to your employees. Find out what non-profits or charities they support and go with them and I will say, they will know you care and then they will fight and work their tails off for you.

Get involved.

It is not a difficult thing to grasp and understand. Invite these non-profits or charities into the workplace to talk for 30 minutes on what they are doing and how they can be your partner. Do this once a week and it will work wonders getting you into the community and you will meet some incredible and beautiful people.

Sponsor little league teams, get into the schools and reward those who are excelling on and off the field, and work with animal and rescue shelters across the area.

And on and on and on and on.

I can only speak about my previous work life, but going once a year to plant trees or clean up a park, that is not getting involved, no matter how hard you try to spin it. And boy, did you try to spin it.

Get involved. There is simply no wrong answer here and in the end, you will love every single second of doing it and meeting people who will positively impact your life.

After all, why do you think everyone is moving here?

CHAPTER 10

Let's start out by saying I am far from perfect. Far. As in the Sun to Jupiter far. Or 65 south on the interstate from Rivergate to Nashville stuck in rush hour traffic far. (That is probably a far better comparison.)

So when it comes to judging someone, I am not the best person to be doing it but after what I saw one recent evening at the grocery store, I had to do it.

I have always been mesmerized by those who will not put a grocery cart back where it belongs. I am not talking about walking it all the way back into the store but there are slots in the parking lot that are usually pretty close to where you are and it takes minimal effort to put them back.

For example, saw a gentleman who parked close to me and after he unloaded his groceries, left his cart in a parking spot between us. I had to know why.

"Excuse me, but are you going to just leave this here?"

"Why do you care?"

"Why don't you care?"

He reluctantly grabbed the cart and walked it over and with all his might, slammed the cart into the rack.

I started thinking about successful people and whether or not, they would put their cart up. Not billionaire's, but those who have succeeded in life and their career and if a simple act such as returning or putting up a cart, really mattered to them.

For some reason, I think it matters. I had football coaches forever tell me that if you take care of the small things, the big things will take care of themselves.

There was a viral moment in a Dallas Cowboys football game where quarterback Dak Prescott was throwing away a paper cup and missed the trash can. He then got up, went and picked up the cup and tossed it away. Took about 4 seconds and I became a big fan after that. He didn't have to do that but the little things matter and I am sure his mom instilled that in him.

The great Don Meyer always said, "Leave things better than you found them." Simple sentence but oh so powerful in every single way. Returning a shopping cart is something that is simple and shows character to walk it back to where it belongs.

It really is not rocket science but after seeing carts at the bottom of the parking lot, time and time again, maybe it is.

OK, we got this now let me go inside and let's figure out how to self scan our items in a timely manner. This may take awhile.

THANK YOU

I sincerely hope and pray these simple things can change your life for the better in so many ways. They work because I applied them to my life and I have seen the results.

I will leave you all with this. When I was 27, I decided to go back to college and get my degree. I had a lot of consternation about being too old and out of touch. God kept telling me to go, just go and it will be okay.

My first day at Middle Tennessee State University, an ice storm had hit the campus two days before. School was delayed a day and I had an 8 A.M. class and I was walking underneath the football stadium to get there, I slipped and fell on the ice. Hard.

It felt like five minutes of trying not to fall but it was about 5 seconds. I ended up falling flat on my face. I looked up and there were at least eight people staring at me.

At that moment though, I knew I would be all right. Had no doubt. Why, you ask. Here is why——I fell forward. Yes, I fell on my face, but I still fell forward. Not backwards, but forward.

I knew then, nothing was going to stop me. Thank you, Lord.

I will leave you with my favorite bible verse that is another example that God wants us all to succeed.

Luke 11:9.

Now go create that chaos.

SPECIAL THANKS

My Lord and Savior, Jesus Christ, who I am sure, shakes His head daily at my antics.

My children, Hannah and J.J. I have been called a lot of things in my life but Dad is the best.

To my mom above, I will see you again and we have a lot to catch up on.

My brother Ric, I couldn't have anyone more important in my corner than you. Thanks for saving my tail more times than I can count.

SOS. Forever

Made in the USA
Monee, IL
17 September 2022